KU-431-279

With A
Grateful
Heart

With A Grateful Heart

THE
JOY OF
THANKSGIVING

written and compiled by
Bonnie Harvey

BARBOUR
PUBLISHING, INC.
Uhrichsville, Ohio

© MCMXCIX by Barbour Publishing, Inc.

ISBN 1-57748-463-3

All Scripture quotations are taken from the King James Version of the Bible.

Published by Barbour Publishing, Inc., P.O. Box 719, Uhrichsville, OH 44683 http://www.barbourbooks.com

 Member of the
Evangelical Christian
Publishers Association

Printed in the United States of America.

THE BLESSING OF GIVING THANKS

(THE ART OF THANKSGIVING)

Giving thanks always for all things
unto God and the Father
in the name of our Lord Jesus Christ.

EPHESIANS 5:20

Father,
with everything else You've given me,
grant me a grateful heart.

HYMN OF THANKSGIVING

Let all things now living,
    a song of thanksgiving
To God the Creator triumphantly raise,
    Who fashioned and made us,
        protected and stayed us,
Who guideth us on to the end of our days.

His banners are o'er us,
    His light goes before us,
A pillar of fire shining forth in the night,
    'Til shadows have vanished
And darkness is banished,
    As forward we travel from light into light.

His law He enforces:
    The stars in their courses,
The sun in His orbit, obediently shine;
    The hills and the mountains,
The rivers and fountains,
    The deeps of the ocean proclaim Him divine.

We, too, should be voicing
    our love and rejoicing,
With glad adoration a song let us raise,
    'Til all things now living
        unite in thanksgiving
To God in the highest, hosanna and praise!

GIVING THANKS

For three things I thank God every day of my
life:
    thanks that He has vouchsafed me
        knowledge of His works;
    deep thanks that He has set
        in my darkness the lamp of faith;
    deep, deepest thanks that I have
        another life to look forward to—
a life joyous with light and flowers
        and heavenly song.

HELEN ADAMS KELLER

Lord,
teach me to count my blessings—
large and small.

A PSALM OF
PRAISE AND THANKSGIVING

O come, let us sing unto the LORD:
let us make a joyful noise
to the rock of our salvation.
Let us come before his presence
with thanksgiving,
and make a joyful noise unto him with psalms.
For the LORD is a great God,
and a great King above all gods.
In his hand are the deep places of the earth:
the strength of the hills is his also.
The sea is his, and he made it:
and his hands formed the dry land.
O come, let us worship and bow down:
let us kneel before the LORD our maker.
For he is our God;
and we are the people of his pasture,
and the sheep of his hand.

PSALM 95:1–7

*God has two dwellings; one in heaven,
and the other in a meek and thankful heart.*

IZAAK WALTON

GEORGE WASHINGTON'S
THANKSGIVING PROCLAMATION

THANKSGIVING AS A HOLIDAY

(A NATIONAL RECOGNITION
OF GOD'S BLESSING)

GEORGE WASHINGTON'S THANKSGIVING PROCLAMATION

In 1784, because the American colonists were so grateful that the Revolutionary War was ended, a special Thanksgiving Day was observed. Five years later, in 1789, President George Washington issued the first Thanksgiving Proclamation of the new nation, the United States of America. Some of the words in his proclamation are these:

Now therefore I do recommend and assign Thursday the twenty-sixth day of November next to be devoted by the People of these States to the service of that great and glorious Being. . . That we may then all unite in rendering unto Him our sincere and humble thanks for His kind care and protection of the People of this country previous to their becoming a Nation, for the single and manifold mercies. . .which we experienced in the course and conclusion of the late war, for the great tranquility, union, and plenty, which we have enjoyed. . .and in general for all the great and various favors which he hath been pleased to confer upon us.

ABRAHAM LINCOLN'S THANKSGIVING PROCLAMATION, 1863

It is the duty of nations as well as of men to own their dependence upon the overruling power of God; to confess their sins and transgressions in humble sorrow, yet with assured hope that genuine repentance will lead to mercy and pardon; and to recognize the sublime truth, announced in the Holy Scriptures and proven by all history, that those nations are blessed whose God is the Lord.

It has seemed to me fit and proper that God should be solemnly, reverently, and gratefully acknowledged, as with one heart and voice, by the whole American people. I do therefore invite my fellow citizens in every part of the United States, and also those who are at sea and those who are sojourning in foreign lands, to set apart and observe the last Thursday of November as a day of Thanksgiving and praise to our beneficent Father who dwelleth in the heavens.

In every thing give thanks:
for this is the will of God
in Christ Jesus concerning you.

1 THESSÁLONIANS 5:18

GIVE THANKS

For all that God, in mercy, sends;
For health and children, home and friends;
For comfort in the time of need,
For every kindly word and deed,
For happy thoughts and holy talk,
For guidance in our daily walk—
    For everything give thanks!

For beauty in this world of ours,
For verdant grass and lovely flowers,
For song of birds, for hum of bees,
For the refreshing summer breeze,
For hill and plain, for stream and wood,
For the great ocean's mighty flood—
    For everything give thanks!

For the sweet sleep which comes with night,
For the returning morning's light,
For the bright sun that shines on high,
For the stars glittering in the sky—
For these, and everything we see,
O Lord! our hearts we lift to Thee—
    For everything give thanks!

ANONYMOUS

Why the Pilgrims Celebrated Thanksgiving in 1621

September 6, 1620. Being thus arrived in a good harbor, and brought safe to land, they fell upon their knees and blessed the God of Heaven who had brought them over the vast and furious ocean, and delivered them from all the perils and miseries thereof, again to set their feet on the firm and stable earth. . . . Being thus passed the vast ocean, and a sea of troubles before in their preparation, they had now no friends to welcome them, nor inns to entertain or refresh their weather-beaten bodies, no houses or much less towns to repair to, to seek for succour. It is recorded in Scripture as a mercy to the Apostle and his shipwrecked company that the barbarians showed them no small kindness in refreshing them, but these savage barbarians, when they met with them, were readier to fill their sides full of arrows.

And for the season it was winter, and they that know the winters of that country know them to be sharp and violent, and subject to cruel and fierce storms, dangerous to travel to known places, much more to search an unknown coast. Besides, what could they see but a hideous and desolate wilderness, full of wild beasts and wild men—and what multitudes there might be of them they knew not. . . . Which way soever they turned their eyes (save upward to the heavens) they could have little solace or content to respect of any outward objects. For summer being done, all things stand upon them with a weather-beaten face, and the whole country, full of woods and thickets, represented a wild and savage hue. If they looked behind them, there was the mighty ocean they had passed and was now as a main bar and gulf to separate them from all the civil parts of the world. What could now sustain them but the Spirit of God and His grace? May not and ought not the children of these fathers rightly say: "Our fathers were Englishmen which came over this great ocean and were ready to perish in this wilderness; but they cried unto the Lord, and He heard their voice and looked on their adversity. Let them therefore praise the Lord because He is good: and His mercies endure forever."

WILLIAM BRADFORD
Governor of Plymouth Plantation,
from his book *Of Plymouth Plantation*

O GOD,
BENEATH THY GUIDING HAND

O God, beneath Thy guiding hand
  Our exiled fathers crossed the sea;
And when they trod the wintry strand,
  With prayer and psalm they worshiped Thee.

Thou heardest, well pleased, the song, the prayer:
  Thy blessing came; and still its power
Shall onward, through all ages, bear
  The memory of that holy hour.

Laws, freedom, truth, and faith in God
  Came with those exiles o'er the waves;
And, where their pilgrim feet have trod,
  The God they trusted guards their graves.

And here Thy name, O God of love,
  Their children's children shall adore,
Till these eternal hills remove,
  And spring adorns the earth no more.

Amen

NOT ALONE FOR MIGHTY EMPIRE

Not alone for mighty empire,
    stretching far over land and sea,
Not alone for bounteous harvests,
    lift we up our hearts to Thee.
Standing in the living present,
    memory and hope between,
Lord, we would with deep thanksgiving,
    praise Thee more for things unseen.
Not for battleships and fortress,
    not for conquests of the sword,
But for conquests of the spirit give we thanks
    to Thee, O Lord;
For the priceless gift of freedom,
    for the home, the church, the school,
For the open door to manhood,
    in a land the people rule.
For the armies of the faithful,
    souls that passed and left no name;
For the glory that illumines patriot lives
    of deathless fame.
For our prophets and apostles,
    loyal to the living Word,
For all heroes of the spirit, give we thanks
    to Thee, O Lord.

WILLIAM PIERSON MERRILL

A Child's Thanksgiving List

1. A house to live in
2. Furniture
3. Our books
4. Education
5. A church to go to
6. Food
7. A school to go to
8. Having accepted Jesus
9. Clothes
10. Parents who believe in Jesus
11. For electricity
12. A library
13. That we have Bibles
14. For our dog, Scottie
15. Plants
16. God
17. That God loves me
18. That my parents don't abuse me
19. I have nice teachers
20. My bug collection; my rock collection
21. That I'm happy
22. For my bicycle—and that it hasn't rusted (yet!)
23. For my new boots
24. That Mrs. Beech's class sold over 100 boxes in the contest
25. That my parents spank me!

SAMUEL F., 11 YEARS OLD

Shouldn't each of us make
our own list of things to be thankful for—
today and every day?
And, don't overlook the small things
like being able to get up each morning,
for the gift of a brand-new day,
and for work to do.

THANKSGIVING DAY

Over the river and through the wood,
To Grandmother's house we go;
The horse knows the way
To carry the sleigh
Through the white and drifted snow.

Over the river and through the wood—
Oh, how the wind does blow!
It stings the toes
And bites the nose,
As over the ground we go.

Over the river and through the wood,
To have a first-rate play.
Hear the bells ring,
Ting-a-ling-ding!
Hurrah for Thanksgiving Day!

Over the river and through the wood
Trot fast, my dapple-gray!
Spring over the ground
Like a hunting-hound!
For this is Thanksgiving Day.

Over the river and through the wood,
And straight through the barnyard gate.
We seem to go
Extremely slow—
It is so hard to wait!

Over the river and through the wood—
Now Grandmother's cap I spy!
Hurrah for the fun!
Is the pudding done?
Hurrah for the pumpkin pie!

LYDIA MARIE CHILD

THANKSGIVING TIME

When all the leaves are off the boughs,
  And nuts and apples gathered in,
And cornstalks waiting for the cows,
  And pumpkins safe in barn and bin;

Then Mother says: "My children dear,
  The fields are brown, and
Autumn flies; Thanksgiving Day is very near,
  And we must make Thanksgiving pies!"

UNKNOWN

MEAL TIME

For what we are about to receive,
  O Lord, make us truly thankful.

Be present at our table, Lord;
  Be here and everywhere adored.

Thy creatures bless and grant that we
  May feast in paradise with Thee.

SIGNIFICANCE OF
THANKSGIVING DAY

The American Thanksgiving is the first such holiday in the world to become a legal holiday. After tracing the history of Thanksgiving back to the Pilgrims, present Americans can better understand why and how the observance developed in our country. Thanksgiving is celebrated as a family day, and aside from Christmas and Easter, it is the only national holiday in our calendar with religious significance. This day, perhaps more than any other day of the whole year, is a day when we can be thankful to God—the Great Provider—for all His goodness and blessings to us.

But my God shall supply all your need according to his riches in glory by Christ Jesus.

PHILIPPIANS 4:19

A PSALM OF PRAISE

Make a joyful noise unto the LORD,
    all ye lands.
Serve the LORD with gladness:
    come before his presence with singing.
Know ye that the LORD he is God:
    it is he that hath made us,
    and not we ourselves;
    we are his people,
    and the sheep of his pasture.
Enter into his gates with thanksgiving,
    and into his courts with praise:
    be thankful unto him,
    and bless his name.
For the LORD is good;
    his mercy is everlasting;
    and his truth endureth to all generations.

PSALM 100

Lord, how we thank You
for the courage of the Pilgrims
to face many difficulties
so they could worship You in freedom.
We also thank You for the opportunities
we have today to worship You
in peace in our land.

ALL IN
A WORD

T   for time to be together, turkey, talk,
and tangy weather.

H   for harvest stored away, home, and
hearth, and holiday.

A   for autumn's frosty art, and abundance
in the heart.

N   for neighbors, and November, nice-
things, new-things to remember.

K   for kitchen, kettles croon—with kith
and kin expected soon.

S   for sizzles, sights, and sounds, and
something-special that abounds.

That spells THANKS. . .for joy of living and a
jolly good Thanksgiving.

AILEEN FISHER

THANKSGIVING AND HARVEST

(REMEMBERING GOD'S
BOUNTIFUL PROVISION)

COME,
YE THANKFUL PEOPLE COME

Come, ye thankful people come,
Raise the song of harvest home!
All is safely gathered in,
Ere the winter storms begin;
God our Maker doth provide
For our wants to be supplied:
Come to God's own temple, come,
Raise the song of harvest home.

All the world is God's own field,
Fruit unto His praise to yield;
Wheat and tares together sown
Unto joy or sorrow grown;
First the blade, and then the ear,
Then the full corn shall appear;
Lord of harvest! grant that we
Wholesome grain and pure may be.

For the Lord our God shall come,
And shall take His harvest home;
From His field shall in that day
All offenses purge away,
Give His angels charge at last
In the fires the tares to cast,
But the fruitful ears to store
In His garner evermore.

Even so, Lord, quickly come,
To Thy final harvest home;
Gather Thou Thy people in,
Free from sorrow, free from sin,
There forever purified,
In Thy presence to abide:
Come, with all Thine angels, come,
Raise the glorious harvest home. Amen.

HENRY ALFORD

Praise to God, Immortal Praise

Praise to God, immortal praise,
   For the love that crowns our days;
Bounteous Source of every joy,
   Let Thy praise our tongues employ.

Flocks that whiten all the plain;
   Yellow sheaves of ripened grain;
Clouds that drop their fattening dews,
   Suns that temperate warmth diffuse.

All that Spring with bounteous hand
   Scatters o'er the smiling land;
All that liberal Autumn pours
   From her rich o'erflowing stores.

These to Thee, my God, we owe,
   Source whence all our blessings flow;
And for these my soul shall raise
   Grateful vows and solemn praise.

ANNA LAETITIA AIKIN BARBAULD

HARVEST-TIME

The joy that eight-year-old Mary felt knew no bounds. The excitement of going to her grandparents' farm for the annual threshing event surpassed even getting a new doll earlier that year. Her grandparents lived on a huge 360-acre farm in the upper Midwest, and each year in late September or early October the crop of oats had to be gathered in.

The early fall weather had been sunny, although a few showers had slowed the harvesting down. Now the farmers were anxious to complete their work so the harvest would not be spoiled. For the threshing, several neighboring farmers would get together. They would bundle the grain into shocks which would then be loaded onto wagons and hauled to the stationary threshing machine.

Mary awoke early the first day of threshing. Her father had promised to take her to the farm, and she knew everyone would be up and about as soon as the sun arose. She didn't want to miss any of this wonderful day. When she arrived, she asked her grandmother, "Grandma, can I help you with anything?"

Her grandmother looked at the little dark-haired girl, small for her age, and nearly said without thinking, "No, I believe all the food is being prepared, and everything else has been looked after." But then, she stopped, noting the wistfulness in her small granddaughter's face— and the earnestness that she saw there caused her to reply: "Well, I reckon you can stir that pot of beans on the stove so's they don't burn." Gladly Mary dragged the rickety kitchen stool in front of the stove, caught up the wooden ladle, and began to stir the huge pot of beans.

Soon, other farmers' wives arrived with their bounty: ham, turkey, roast beef, squash casseroles, creamed corn, candied yams, green beans, and other vegetables and mixed salads. Others brought pumpkin, mince, and apple pies with just-right browned crusts; then someone brought a chocolate cake and a yellow-layer cake. Oh, my, it all looked so good!

Long row tables had been set up in the backyard, and the food placed on one of them. The other table would be where the people, including sons and daughters of the farmers, would be able to sit and eat their meal. Now Mary went to work helping to carry food to the table—and she and some of the Smith children worked at arranging the silverware at each place.

Mary listened to her grandpa, Fred, talking to one of the farmers: "Good crop this year, Albert. Kind of renews my faith in farming. After the poor showing we had last year and even the year before that, I thought I might have to quit after all these years."

Albert spoke up: "Yep, I know what you mean. We have much to be thankful to the good Lord for the huge crop this year. I'll be able to pay off some of my debts from last year. The weather's been pretty for the harvest, too."

A little shiver went through Mary as she thanked God for His goodness to her grandparents. As the day wore on, the farmers took turns eating from the laden tables, the children helped as they could, and the wives stayed busy supplying fresh food to the table.

At last dusk began to settle over the little community, the day's work in the fields was done, and the farmers began to say "Goodnight." Tomorrow they would work at someone else's farm and continue until all the crop was harvested. Around eight o'clock, Mary's father lifted her up from her grandma's sofa where she had fallen fast asleep. Softly he spoke to Grandma, "It's good that threshin' time comes but once a year. Don't think Mary could take much more of it!" With that, he carried the little girl out to his car for the short trip back to town.

With Thankful Hearts, O Lord, We Come

With thankful hearts, O Lord, we come,
　　To praise Thy name in grateful song;
Accept the offering, Lord, we bring,
　　And help us loud Thy praises sing.

We thank Thee, Lord, for daily food,
　　For plenteous store of earthly good;
For life, and health, we still possess,
　　With house and home so richly blest.

We thank Thee for this goodly land,
　　Where freedom reigns on every hand;
Do Thou, O Lord, our country bless,
　　With heavenly peace and righteousness.

We thank Thee for Thy blessed Word,
　　That to our souls doth life afford;
Help us its message to receive,
　　And from the heart its truth believe.

　　　　　　　　　　　　　　Amen

WE PLOW THE FIELDS

We plow the fields and scatter
   The good seed on the land,
But it is fed and watered
   By God's almighty hand;
He sends the snow in winter,
   The warmth to swell the grain,
The breezes and the sunshine,
   And soft refreshing rain.

He only is the Maker
   Of all things near and far;
He paints the wayside flower,
   He lights the evening star;
The winds and waves obey Him,
   By Him the birds are fed;
Much more to us, His children,
   He gives our daily bread.

We thank Thee, then, O Father,
   For all things bright and good,
The seed-time and the harvest,
   Our life, our health, our food;
Accept the gifts we offer,
   For all Thy love imparts,
And what Thou most desirest,
   Our humble, thankful hearts.

THE CORN SONG

Heap high the farmer's wintry hoard!
Heap high the golden corn!
No richer gift has autumn poured
From out her lavish horn!

Through vales of grass and meads of flowers,
Our ploughs their furrows made,
While on the hills the sun and showers
Of changeful April played.

We dropped the seed o'er hill and plain,
Beneath the sun of May,
And frightened from our sprouting grain
The robber crows away.

All through the long, bright days of June
Its leaves grew green and fair,
And waved in hot midsummer's sun
Its soft and golden hair.

And now, with autumn's moonlit eves,
Its harvest time has come,
We pluck away the frosted leaves
And bear the treasure home.

But let the good old crop adorn
The hills our fathers trod;
Still let us, for His golden corn,
Send up our thanks to God!

JOHN GREENLEAF WHITTIER

While the earth remaineth,
seedtime and harvest,
and cold and heat, and summer and winter,
and day and night shall not cease.

GENESIS 8:22

To Thee, O Lord, Our Hearts We Raise

To Thee, O Lord, our hearts we raise
   in hymns of adoration,
To Thee bring sacrifice of praise
   with shouts of exultation.

Bright robes of gold the fields adorn,
   the hills with joy are ringing,
The valleys stand so thick with corn
   that even they are singing.

And now, on this our festal day,
   Thy bounteous hand confessing,
Upon Thine altar, Lord, we lay
   the firstfruits of Thy blessing.

By Thee all human souls are led
   with gifts of grace supernal;
Thou, Who gives us our daily bread,
   give us the bread eternal.

We bear the burden of the day,
   and often toil seems dreary;
But labor ends with sunset ray,
   and rest comes for the weary.

May we, the angel reaping over,
   stand at the last accepted,
Christ's golden sheaves, forevermore
   to garners bright elected.

O blessèd is that land of God
   where saints abide forever,
Where golden fields spread fair and broad,
   where flows the crystal river.

The strains of all its holy throng
   with ours today are blending;
Thrice blessèd is that harvest song
   which never hath an ending.

WILLIAM CHATTERTON DIX

THANKSGIVING SURPRISE

The delightful drive to their grandparents' house in Connecticut went smoothly enough. The Brown family, Robert and Nancy, and their children, Jane, ten, and Mike, eight, each looked forward to Grandma's wonderful cooking. There was no one who could make a sweet potato pie as good as she could! And, she kept her recipes a secret, too.

A gently falling early snow added to the festive occasion, and as they turned into the familiar driveway, Grandma and Grandpa walked quickly to the car.

"Hi, everybody," greeted Grandpa, as the car doors flew open.

"Happy Thanksgiving!" returned the Browns, all at the same time.

Grandma added, "Dinner's almost ready. Probably just a few more minutes. Come in and hang up your coats before you catch your death of pneumonia out here!"

The Browns fairly ran into the small, cozy New England cottage. Comfortable without being pretentious, the furnishings were mostly "early attic," but suited the grandparents just right. The aromatic smells from the kitchen enveloped the other rooms in the house, and Robert and Nancy smiled at each other in eagerness of what was to come. Just then, Grandma called from the kitchen: "I'm just takin' the turkey out. Come see the big bird!"

So adults and youngsters trooped to the kitchen to watch the big event. Grandma opened the oven door, and the good-sized turkey filled the roasting pan. It looked done to perfection. Then Grandma set it on the counter and prepared to remove the stuffing. Everyone crowded around to see the savory cornbread dressing when Grandma let out a shriek. At the same time, she pulled out a dingy, stuffing-covered dish towel that had baked along with the dressing.

"Well, bless my soul!" she cried. "I can't believe I did such a thing. I was drying dishes when I put the finishing touches on the stuffin'. Guess I got absent-minded with too many things on my mind and dropped the dish towel in with the dressing! Anyone want stuffed dish towel for Thanksgiving dinner?"

The others just stood and grinned. They all had a good laugh over grandma's forgetfulness as they ate Thanksgiving dinner. The incident made that Thanksgiving one of the most memorable ever.

A merry heart doeth good like a medicine.

PROVERBS 17:22

Father, we thank You
for giving us a sense of humor.
Help us not to take ourselves too seriously
and to be able to laugh at ourselves. Amen.

MEDITATIONS ON THANKFULNESS

(EIGHT DAYS OF INSPIRATION DERIVED FROM THE WORD "THANKFUL")

T IS FOR THANKSGIVING

Giving thanks always for all things unto God.
EPHESIANS 5:20

The blessedness of giving thanks to the Lord cannot be overemphasized. Whatever the situation, whether it be filled with joy, or filled with sadness and even despair, we are told to give thanks to God.

Why does the Bible tell us to do such a simple yet often difficult task? To give God thanks, first of all, is an act of worship and obedience—we are commanded to do so. But giving thanks also implies trust in God; trust that He will do what His Word promises; trust that He will answer that seemingly impossible prayer request; and trust that "all things work together for good" (Romans 8:28).

Throughout the Old Testament, particularly in the Psalms, we are told repeatedly to give thanks and praise to God. A good example of this instruction appears in Psalm 50:14–15 where the psalmist reminds us to "Offer unto God thanksgiving; and pay thy vows unto the most High: And call upon me in the day of trouble: I will deliver thee, and thou shalt glorify me." Here we see a direct link between giving thanks to God, calling upon Him in trouble, and then, witnessing His mighty deliverance in and through a difficult place.

When Shadrach, Meshach, and Abednego refused to bow down and worship an earthly king, they were thrown into the fiery furnace. But they trusted God to deliver them—and He did! In fact, they came out of the intense fire and heat without their bodies or clothing being burned, without their hair being singed or even the smell of smoke clinging to them!

As we give thanks to God, something mysterious happens. It is as though we place our hand in His and provide an open door for Him to work. May the Lord help us to be thankful at all times.

H IS FOR HEART

I will praise thee, O LORD,
with my whole heart;
I will show forth all thy marvelous works.
PSALM 9:1

The psalmist's joy in praising the Lord is contagious as he determines to praise the Lord with his whole heart. In essence, the psalmist makes a vow to praise God whether anyone else does or not. Neither will he consider his feelings nor his emotions in the matter; but he will put forth the strength of his will in this high calling of praise.

With enthusiasm, the psalmist also declares that by his will he should be enabled to give whole-hearted praise to the Lord; no halfhearted measures are sufficient. If an athlete running a race wants to win, he must run with his whole being set on the goal. Otherwise, any halfhearted effort guarantees failure. Moreover, whatever occupation a person has, he must pursue it wholeheartedly, or he will not be successful. Would we desire to have a surgeon operate on us if he would not do his best? Or would we have an attorney represent us if he possessed an indifferent attitude? No, whatever our task, we need to do it with quiet determination, yet with confidence and joy knowing that we have done our best.

So with the psalmist, there is no proper way to praise the Lord except with a "whole heart." Having made this declaration, the psalmist adds that he will then show forth all of God's marvelous works.

What are these marveloous works? They're simply God's dealings with each of us, beginning with the work of Christ's salvation. But daily we see the Lord's provision for us in many things: a good night's rest, strength for the day, His watch-care over us in keeping us from harm, our daily bread, family and friends, and overall, His peace and joy.

May the Lord grant us grace to praise Him with our whole heart—and thus to show forth His marvelous works.

A IS FOR ACCEPTABLE

Let the words of my mouth, and the meditation
of my heart, be acceptable in thy sight,
O LORD, my strength, and my redeemer.
PSALM 19:14

The psalmist prays that his words and his thoughts will find favor with the Lord. He knows what we all know too well—that we often speak without thinking; but once we utter the words, we can never call them back. Like flying arrows, they go straight to the mark—whether for good or for ill.

Knowing too well the problem of "taming the tongue," the psalmist cries out to God for help. He does not want to be guilty of hidden and unconscious faults, nor of presumptuous sins (or, willful sins). On the one hand, he speaks of unknown sins; on the other, he addresses the sins he's aware of committing but seems helpless to prevent. He is painfully aware of the too-frequent hypocrisy in his life: For example, he meets a fellow Christian and calls to him, "Good afternoon, Brother Bill. How good it is to see you!" But under his breath, he thinks, "That old reprobate. I hope our paths don't cross again!" His attitude and words are hypocritical and contradict the clear teaching of biblical verses such as 1 Peter 1:22 that says to have "unfeigned love of the brethren."

It's easy for us to identify with the psalmist since we, too, want to say and do the right thing. Because of his sinful nature, however, the psalmist knows he cannot attain to what the Scripture commands by himself. But he rejoices at the close of Psalm 19 as he calls upon the Lord, "my strength, and my redeemer." The Lord can—and will—help him overcome his hypocritical ways. As he seeks the Lord for help, the Lord will render his words and his thoughts acceptable in His sight.

Lord, help us to pray this prayer today—and mean it!

N IS FOR NAME

*O LORD, our Lord, how excellent is thy name
in all the earth!*
PSALM 8:1

If we ask, "What's in a name?" we might get
many different answers. Most of us understand,
however, that the name of a person represents
all that he or she is. The person who bears a
certain name is distinct. No other individual is
identical to that person.

So it is with God; only His name is high above
every other name on earth or in heaven. Further,
the psalmist declares the excellency of the Lord's
name and stresses that God has set His glory
(and His name) above the heavens. We see God's
glory everywhere in creation: in the beauty of a
sunrise and sunset; in the wonder of a budding
flower; in the music of a bird's song; in the
uniqueness of other people; and throughout this
beautiful world that He has made.

When we speak of the meaning of God's
name, consider what the Scripture says: "His
name shall be called Wonderful, Counsellor,
The mighty God, The everlasting Father, The
Prince of Peace" (Isaiah 9:6); "Thou shalt call

his name JESUS: for he shall save his people from their sins" (Matthew 1:21); "They shall call his name Emmanuel, which being interpreted is, God with us" (Matthew 1:23). Also in the New Testament, Jesus declares, "Before Abraham was, I am" (John 8:58). Last of all, in the book of Revelation, the Lord says He is "Alpha and Omega, the beginning and the end," and the "KING OF KINGS, AND LORD OF LORDS."

The amazing fact about the names of the Lord is that He includes us in many of them—and He invites us to use His name in prayer. Truly, He is "God with us."

How thankful we should be to our gracious God for all He has provided for every need; for the wonder of His creation; and that He bids us to "Call upon My name!"

THURSDAY
K IS FOR KEEP

The LORD. . .will not suffer thy foot to be moved: he that keepeth thee will not slumber. Behold, he that keepeth Israel shall neither slumber nor sleep. The LORD is thy keeper.
PSALM 121:2–5

Psalm 121 could well be known as the "Keeping psalm." In fact, nearly every verse in this reassuring psalm uses the word "keep" in one way or the other. To "keep" something implies faithfulness and reliability; the word also speaks of preserving, as in the process of canning fruits and vegetables so they will last a long time.

The psalmist rests secure in the knowledge that God, the Maker of heaven and earth, is watching over him and protecting him. And he has that bedrock assurance that the Lord "orders" every step he takes. None of his footsteps will slip or slide because the Lord holds his feet to the path mapped out for him. Sometimes we think we have missed the way, but as we call on the One Who never slumbers nor sleeps, He will set our feet back on the right pathway. Even as Jonah got on the ship bound for Tarshish and the Lord sent a whale to transport him to Nineveh, the Lord will do the same for us to assure the finishing of our course.

The Lord not only keeps us, but He is our Keeper. The God of the universe has a personal interest in us. Like a gardener tending his garden, the word "keeper" suggests the Lord taking care of every detail that concerns us. In a sense, we are His "keepsakes"! He makes sure the sun does not shine too brightly, nor the moon hide any treachery from us. In short, whether we're coming or going on our daily journey, the Lord oversees every aspect, protecting and caring for us.

Lord, teach us always to lift our eyes to You—from whence our help comes.

F IS FOR FAITHFULNESS

*Thy mercy, O LORD, is in the heavens; and thy
faithfulness reacheth unto the clouds.*
Psalm 36:5

Faithfulness is such a wonderful quality! We prize this characteristic in people above all others. To illustrate, if someone asks a woman to help in a community effort, usually the person who asks her knows she can count on her to fulfill her duties. She already knows the woman to be dependable and reliable; she is faithful. Or, if an organization wants a man to contribute his expertise to a small building project, the committee knows they can depend on him to be there because he said he would be. He keeps his word.

So it is with God. In this verse, the psalmist reaches for the clouds to extol God's faithfulness to us: God's love and faithfulness have no limit. Despite our sinfulness, God's mercy extends way past the sin as His love and compassion toward us attain the very heavens.

The prophet Jeremiah, in Lamentations 3:22–23, declares triumphantly: "It is of the LORD's mercies that we are not consumed, because his compassions fail not. They are new every morning: great is thy faithfulness." What confidence we can have toward the Lord as these words grip us. Even when we say or do wrong things, the Lord's hand is always outstretched toward us. We serve a God whose love is steadfast and unchanging toward us, and we can rest in that knowledge.

The words of the hymn "Great Is Thy Faithfulness" express the Lord's constancy well:

Great is Thy faithfulness, O God my Father!
There is no shadow of turning with Thee;
Thou changest not, Thy compassions, they fail
    not:

As Thou hast been Thou forever wilt be.
Pardon for sin and a peace that endureth,
Thine own dear presence to cheer and to guide,
Strength for today and bright hope for tomorrow—
Blessings all mine, with ten thousand beside!

REFRAIN:
Great is Thy faithfulness! Great is Thy
    faithfulness!
Morning by morning new mercies I see;
All I have needed Thy hand hath provided—
Great is Thy faithfulness, Lord, unto me!

May the Lord help us to be worthy recipients of His faithfulness to us.

U IS FOR UNDERSTANDING

How sweet are thy words unto my taste!
yea, sweeter than honey to my mouth.
Through thy precepts I get understanding:
therefore I hate every false way.
PSALM 119:103–104

The psalmist had learned the secret of meditating in God's Word. To him, the book of the Law was not just another book, but its words contained the very life of God. Thus Jesus reminds us in John 6:63: "The words that I speak unto you, they are spirit, and they are life." These words follow an earlier passage in which Jesus calls Himself "the Bread of Life." In these verses, Jesus, like the psalmist, lets us know the true worth of God's Word.

As He contrasts God's Word with natural food, Jesus illustrates the difference between the flesh and the spirit: Feeding the one leads to death; feeding the other leads to life. Moreover, He teaches us in Matthew 4:4: "It is written, Man shall not live by bread alone, but by every word that proceedeth out of the mouth of God." Jesus answered Satan with these words when the devil commanded Him to turn stones into bread after Jesus' forty-day fast; thus, He provides an example for us to follow.

The psalmist, too, extols his love for God's Word. Through his maturity in the Lord, he can now truthfully exclaim that God's words are "sweeter than honey to my mouth!" Thinking of how sweet honey is on a slice of warm toast or topping cereal in a bowl, we can appreciate what he is saying. When he began his Christian life, he enjoyed the "milk" of God's Word, but now the Word constitutes his "daily bread" and even dessert!

Through his meditation in God's Word, the psalmist has received instruction as well as nourishment. This instruction in guidance, direction, correction, and encouragement shows him how to live according to God's will. By following God's Word, he can avoid the pitfalls of life (every false way)—or, anything that would take him from the path the Lord has for him. By meditating in these truths, the psalmist grows in his understanding of how to conduct his life.

Lord, let Your Word become increasingly sweet to us, and enable us to grow in grace, in knowledge, and in our understanding of You.

SUNDAY
L IS FOR LIGHT

*The LORD is my light and my salvation; whom
shall I fear? the LORD is the strength of my
life; of whom shall I be afraid?*
PSALM 27:1

This verse expresses great hope and encouragement. The psalmist tells of his personal rela-
tionship with the Lord when he says He is "my
light" and "my salvation." At the new birth, we
discover a new light in our lives—a new "light-
ness," peace, and joy in our hearts. We know
that God is real, and that He cares for us. But
that is just the beginning of the Christian life.
Every step of the way, God shines light on the
believer's path. Because of God's light, darkness and gloom disappear; they cannot remain
in His glorious light.

Can you remember being afraid of the dark
when you were a child? You'd thrust your body
down under the sheets, then you'd pull the cov-
ers up over your head. Somehow you thought
the darkness would leave if you couldn't see it.
But if you poked your head out, the darkness
was still there.

Growing up we are taught that darkness hides

all manner of evil. But in and of ourselves, we are helpless to dispel the darkness until our Savior comes to live in our hearts. Light, especially sunlight, is the most important energy in the world. Without it, trees, plants, and flowers could not grow, nor many animals find food and shelter. Even as human beings, we require essential vitamins found in the sun's rays. When we have rainy weather and the sun doesn't shine for days, the farmer's crops are in danger.

How comforting to know that God's light will never dim nor go out, and that we can always walk in its brightness. In addition, Jesus says in John 8:12: "I am the light of the world: he that followeth me shall not walk in darkness, but shall have the light of life." No wonder the psalmist can rejoice in the God Who is not only his Light, but also his Salvation. From start to finish, he has nothing to fear. Thus the psalmist dreads nothing; he finds shelter and safety in the Lord.

How thankful we are that the Lord is our light and our salvation. May we live today in the strength of this knowledge.

Heavenly Father,
help me to be more thankful for all the
wonderful blessings You have so generously
bestowed on me and my loved ones.

THINGS FOR WHICH
WE'RE THANKFUL

(REMINDERS OF GOD'S GOODNESS)

THANKFULNESS

First among the things to be thankful for is a thankful spirit. Some people would grumble at the accommodations in Heaven if they ever got there. They take their blessings here so much as a matter of course, that even a day of general thanksgiving once in a year is more than they feel any need of. And if their personal blessings in any measure fail, gratitude for what they have had or still enjoy is the last thing they think of.

How different with the thankful heart! What a gift it is to be born with an outlook toward the bright side of things! And if not so by nature, what a triumph of grace to be made thankful through a renewed heart! It is so much more comfortable and rational to see what we have to be thankful for and to rejoice accordingly, than to have our vision forever filled with our lacks and our needs. Happy are they who possess this gift! Blessings may fail and fortunes vary, but the thankful heart remains. The happy past, at least, is secure—and Heaven is ahead.

TRUE FREEDOM

And you shall know the truth,
and the truth shall make you free.

JOHN 8:32

WORSHIP

The hour cometh, and now is,
when the true worshippers shall worship
the Father in spirit and in truth:
for the Father seeketh such to worship him.
God is a Spirit: and they that worship
him must worship him in spirit and in truth.

JOHN 4:23–24

THE SPIRIT OF GIVING

John and his eleven-year-old son had frequently helped to serve needy people in their church food pantry. This year, the evening before Thanksgiving, the church had received the names of fifteen families who needed food baskets. One of the local grocers had donated hams and turkeys, and the church bought groceries from a neighborhood discount food distributor.

As each one from the church packed his or her basket for the families, an anticipation grew for the families who would receive the food. The church hall overflowed with food items, and the people preparing the baskets became increasingly excited. Many of these families probably hadn't had enough to eat in some time. No doubt their Thanksgiving dinner would be the best meal they had enjoyed in recent days.

Soon, the families began to arrive to pick up their baskets. Then, a new family appeared: A father, mother, and three children drove up in a battered old Chevy. They had just learned that the church was giving away food—would they be able to get some?

They were new to the area, and the father had not worked in awhile. As Jake, the person in charge, tried to tell the family that there were exactly the right number of baskets for the fifteen families and nothing extra, a man on the other side of the fellowship hall put his basket down and began to take canned items from it, placing them in a box he quickly located. Before long, others in the room imitated him until the good-sized box was filled with the new family's Thanksgiving dinner.

Quietly, a spirit of love and joy invaded the fellowship hall as each participant in the little drama rejoiced that they, too, had been able to be a part of someone else's Thanksgiving.

Blessings Often Overlooked

1. God loves us
2. He forgives our sins
3. He answers prayer
4. The comfort and security of home
5. The kindness of strangers
6. Friends who love us
7. Family members who love us
   (and accept us)
8. Health—and the health of loved ones
9. Regaining health and strength after an illness
10. Work to do
11. A sense of well-being
12. The smell of food cooking—
    especially when you're hungry!
13. Solving a problem or difficulty
14. Making a good decision
15. Renewed hope
16. A good night's rest
17. Money to pay bills!
18. Enjoying your family and friends
19. Reading a good article or book
20. Visiting a place of history or beauty
21. Learning new things
22. Feasting your eyes on the beauties of nature
23. Watching a sunrise—or a sunset
24. When all is quiet outside, hearing sounds
    from the little night creatures
25. Walking in crisp, autumn air

OBSERVATION

The first wealth is health.

RALPH WALDO EMERSON

Father, we thank You that
Your grace is sufficient for us,
and that we can be content with
such things as You give us.
Deliver us from covetousness.

CONTENTMENT

Let your conversation be without covetousness; and be content with such things as you have; for he hath said, I will never leave you nor forsake thee. But godliness with contentment is great gain. For we brought nothing into this world, and it is certain we can carry nothing out. And having food and raiment let us be therewith content.

HEBREWS 13:5; 1 TIMOTHY 6:6–8

WISE COUNSEL

When I would beget content, and increase confidence in the power and wisdom and providence of Almighty God, I will walk in the meadows of some gliding stream, and there contemplate the lilies that take no care, and those very many other little living creatures that are not only created, but fed (a man knows not how) by the goodness of the God of Nature, and therefore trust in Him.

IZAAK WALTON

PRAYER

O friends! with whom my feet have trod
    The quiet aisles of prayer.
Glad witness to your zeal for God
    And love of man I bear.

Yet in the maddening maze of things,
    And tossed by storm and flood,
To one fixed trust my spirit clings;
    I know that God is good. . . .

And Thou, O Lord! by Whom are seen
    Thy creatures as they be,
Forgive me if too close I lean
    My human heart on Thee!

JOHN GREENLEAF WHITTIER

Fellowship

As I traveled to Chosica, Peru, some time ago to work with the Quechua Indians at a mission compound, I wondered what the trip would be like. I knew it would involve getting up early and also a lot of hard work since we planned to help with a building project. I also realized from a previous mission trip to Ecuador that even a sleeping bag looks good at night when you're exhausted from doing physical labor!

We flew into Lima but it was very late at night, so we were unable to see much of the city. Then our hosts took us immediately on to Chosica, which is about an hour's drive from Lima, and right in the heart of the Andes Mountains.

There were twenty-six in our group, including some hard-working teenagers, and since we got settled very late that first night, we decided to go to a church service on Sunday afternoon instead of the following morning. By way of introduction to a new country, our host led us on a walking tour of downtown Chosica on Sunday. What a beautiful place it was with the mountains ringing the city, beautiful blue skies, and a very dry, desert climate. The June temperature stayed around seventy-five degrees day in and day out—although the nights would get much cooler. And it never rained! To be in a place where it (practically) never rained seemed very odd to all of us.

We greatly enjoyed the tour of downtown Chosica with its great open square in the city's center and many lovely flower beds bordering the pathways. A band was playing, and families strolled along the sidewalks. Sunday is a day for families in many South American countries, and they spend the day together. On our tour we also passed a huge outdoor market that sold all types of fruits and vegetables—but other markets (and stores) sold various kinds of merchandise. Many dogs roamed the streets—the natives eat their meat at these markets.

By early afternoon, we needed to get ready for a Quechua church service. Many of us walked to the church which was quite high up on the side of a mountain along a dusty trail. What a surprise when we got to the church! It had no walls, some type of canvas roof that blew in the breeze, and an uneven dirt floor. The Indian congregation let us use the rough-hewn wooden benches to sit on; some of them sat on the floor or on a low wall that bordered one side.

The service began at 3:00 and lasted for close to three hours, and we all sang and clapped our hands even though we didn't understand the language! The sermon and the songs were a mixture of Quechuan and Spanish. The love and acceptance each of us felt from these humble people was overwhelming. Some of our group gave personal testimonies which were then translated into the Quechuan language. The Indians just grinned and clapped in approval.

Following the service, we learned that the women had prepared a meal for us. They had spent at least six hours cooking, in their primitive fashion, a meal consisting of chicken, potatoes, beans, and corn-on-the-cob. (At first, we looked to our hosts about eating the food because you can become very ill eating food in a foreign country—but they said it was okay!)

The meal was a real treat—and an honor. For these people to give us, complete strangers to them, a wonderful meal that no doubt cost them quite a lot, was overwhelming.

Even though we didn't speak the same verbal language, the Quechua Indians communicated the love of Christ through providing a meal for us and giving us what they had. That day, in Chosica, Peru, each one in our group experienced anew the true fellowship of believers.

REAL CHRISTIANITY

Christianity is not a voice in the wilderness, but
    a life in the world.
It is not an idea in the air but feet on the ground,
    going God's way.
It is not an exotic to be kept under glass, but a
    hardy plant to bear twelve
months of fruits in all kinds of weather. Fidelity
    to duty is its root and branch.
Nothing we can say to the Lord, no calling Him
    by great or dear names,
can take the place of the plain doing of His will.
    We may cry out about the
beauty of eating bread with Him in His king-
    dom, but it is wasted breath and
a rootless hope, unless we plow and plant in
    His kindom here and now. To remember
Him at His table and to forget Him at ours, is to
    have invested in bad securities.
There is no substitute for plain, every-day
    goodness.

MALTBIE BABCOCK

Sermons We See

I'd rather see a sermon
   than hear one any day,
I'd rather one should walk with me
   than merely show the way.
The eye's a better pupil
   and more willing than the ear;
Fine counsel is confusing,
   but example's always clear;
And the best of all the preachers are
   the men who live their creeds,
For to see the good in action
   is what everybody needs.
I can soon learn how to do it
   if you'll let me see it done.
I can watch your hands in action,
   but your tongue too fast may run.
And the lectures you deliver
   may be very wise and true;
But I'd rather get my lesson
   by observing what you do.
For I may misunderstand you
   and the high advice you give.
But there's no misunderstanding
   how you act and how you live.

Edgar A. Guest

FRIENDS

Tears glistened in the eyes of Salvation Army officer Shaw as he looked at the three men in front of him. Shaw was a medical missionary who had just arrived in India. It was the turn of the century, and the Salvation Army was taking over the care of the leper colony.

But these three lepers had manacles and fetters binding their hands and feet, cutting the diseased flesh. Captain Shaw turned to the guard and said, "Please unfasten the chains."

"It isn't safe," the guard replied. "These men are dangerous criminals as well as lepers."

"I'll be responsible. They're suffering enough," Captain Shaw said, as he put out his hand and took the keys. Then he knelt on the ground, tenderly removed the shackles, and treated their bleeding ankles.

About two weeks later Captain Shaw had his first misgivings about freeing the criminals. He had to make an overnight trip and dreaded leaving his wife and child alone.

The next morning when she went to her front door, she was startled to see the three criminals lying on her steps.

One explained, "We know doctor go. We stay here so no harm come to you." This was how "dangerous men" responded to an act of love.

EVELYN WICK SMITH

MIRACLES

Why, who makes much of a miracle?
As to me I know of nothing else but miracles,
Whether I walk the streets of Manhattan,
Or dart my sight over the roofs of houses
    toward the sky,
Or wade with naked feet along the beach just
    in the edge of the water,
Or stand under the trees in the woods,
Or talk by day with any one I love, or sleep in
    the bed at night with the one I love,
Or sit at the table at dinner with the rest,
Or look at strangers opposite me riding in the
    car,
Or watch honey-bees busy around the hive of
    a summer forenoon,
Or animals feeding in the fields,
Or birds, or the wonderfulness of insects in
    the air,
Or the wonderfulness of the sundown, or of
    stars shining so quiet and bright,
Or the exquisite delicate thin curve of the new
    moon in spring;

These with the rest, one and all, are to me
    miracles,
The whole referring, yet each distinct and in
    its place,
To me every hour of the light and dark is a
    miracle,
Every cubic inch of space is a miracle,
Every square yard of the surface of the earth is
    spread with the same,
Every foot of the interior swarms with the
    same.
To me the sea is a continual miracle,
The fishes that swim—the rocks—the motion
    of the waves—the ships with men in them,
What stranger miracles are there?

WALT WHITMAN

PROVIDENCE

By going a few minutes sooner or later, by stopping to speak with a friend on the corner, by meeting this man or that, or by turning down this street instead of the other, we may let slip some impending evil, by which the whole current of our lives would have been changed. There is no possible solution in the dark enigma, but the one word "Providence."

HENRY WADSWORTH LONGFELLOW

LIFE AND LOVE

What delightful hosts are they—
Life and Love!
Lingeringly I turn away,
This late hour, yet glad enough
They have not withheld from me
Their high hospitality.
So, with face lit with delight
And all gratitude, I stay
Yet to press their hands and say,
"Thanks—so fine a time! Good night."

JAMES WHITCOMB RILEY

THE GIFT OF LIFE

Life is a gift to be used every day,
Not to be smothered and hidden away;
It isn't a thing to be stored in the chest
Where you gather your keepsakes and treasure
    your best;
It isn't a joy to be sipped now and then
And promptly put back in a dark place again.

Life is a gift that the humblest may boast of
And one that the humblest may well make the
    most of.
Get out and live it each hour of the day,
Wear it and use it as much as you may;
Don't keep it in niches and corners and
    grooves,
You'll find that in service its beauty improves.

EDGAR A. GUEST

Lord, thank You for the gift of life.
Help us to use wisely the gifts and talents You
have given each one of us.

Thanksgiving Miscellany

(A Potpourri of Gratitude)

A Prayer of Thanksgiving

Lord, behold our family here assembled.
We thank Thee
For this place in which we dwell;
For the peace accorded us this day,
For the hope with which we expect tomorrow;
For the health, the work, the food
And the bright skies that make our lives
    delightful,
For our friends in all parts of the earth, and our
    friendly helpers. . .
Let peace abound in our small company.

ROBERT LOUIS STEVENSON

NOW THANK WE ALL OUR GOD

Now thank we all our God
   With heart and hands and voices,
Who wondrous things hath done,
   In whom His world rejoices;
Who from our mothers' arms,
   Hath blessed us on our way
With countless gifts of love,
   And still is ours today.

O may this bounteous God
   Through all our life be near us,
With ever joyful hearts
   And blessed peace to cheer us;
And keep us in His grace,
   And guide us when perplexed,
And free us from all ills
   In this world and the next.

All praise and thanks to God
   The Father now be given,
The Son, and Him who reigns
   With Them in highest heaven—
The one eternal God,
   Whom earth and heaven adore—
For thus it was, is now,
   And shall be evermore. Amen.

MARTIN RINKART

Always Being Thankful

None of us is ever too busy to pay his way. It takes only a few seconds to say a heartwarming "Thank you." Probably no American of modern times lived a more hurried or hectic life than Theodore Roosevelt. Yet even on political campaign trips, when in the hustle and bustle he might have been excused from thinking of other people, it was his custom as he left his private train to stop and thank the engineer and fireman for a safe and comfortable trip. It took but a fraction of a minute of his time, but he had two more friends for the rest of his life.

"Good politics," you may say. But good living too—for after all, isn't having friends the basis of happy living, as well as of successful politics?

Nor have I found any situation in which thanks cannot be given. You can thank even total strangers with a nod of the head, a gesture of the hand, a grateful glance—in jostling street crowds, in swaying subway trains, at the theater, in the quiet of a church service, anywhere at all, if your heart is saying, "Thank you."

D. Dunn

FATHER IN HEAVEN, WE THANK THEE

For flowers that bloom about our feet,
　　For tender grass, so fresh and sweet,
For song of bird and hum of bee,
　　For all things fair we hear or see—
Father in heaven, we thank Thee!

For blue of stream, for blue of sky,
　　For pleasant shade of branches high,
For fragrant air and cooling breeze,
　　For beauty of the blowing trees—
Father in heaven, we thank Thee!

For mother-love, for father-care,
　　For brothers strong and sisters fair,
For love at home and school each day,
　　For guidance lest we go astray—
Father in heaven, we thank Thee!

For Thy dear, everlasting arms;
　　That bear us o'er all ills and harms,
For blessed words of long ago,
　　That help us now Thy will to know—
Father in heaven, we thank Thee!

UNKNOWN

MY GOD, I THANK THEE

My God, I thank Thee, Who hast made
   The earth so bright,
So full of splendor and of joy,
   Beauty and light;
So many glorious things are here,
   Noble and right.

I thank Thee, too, that Thou hast made
   Joy to abound;
So many gentle thoughts and deeds
   Circling us round,
That in the darkest spot of earth
   Some love is found.

I thank Thee more that all our joy
   Is touched with pain,
That shadows fall on brightest hours,
   That thorns remain;
So that earth's bliss may be our guide,
   And not our chain.

For Thou Who knowest, Lord, how soon
   Our weak heart clings,
Hast given us joys, tender and true,
   Yet all with wings;
So that we see gleaming on high
   Dimmer things.

I thank Thee, Lord, that Thou hast kept
   The best in store;
We have enough, yet not too much
   To long for more:
A yearning for a deeper peace
   Not known before.

I thank Thee, Lord, that here our souls,
   Though amply blessed,
Can never find, although they seek,
   A perfect rest;
Nor ever shall, until they lean
   On Jesus' breast.

ADELAIDE ANNE PROCTOR

WITH GRATEFUL HEART
MY THANKS I BRING

With grateful heart my thanks I bring,
Before the great Thy praise I sing;
I worship in Thy holy place
And praise Thee for Thy truth and grace;
For truth and grace together shine
In Thy most holy Word divine,
In Thy most holy Word divine.

I cried to Thee and Thou didst save,
Thy Word of grace new courage gave;
The kings of earth shall thank Thee, Lord,
For they have heard Thy wondrous Word;
Yea, they shall come with songs of praise,
For great and glorious are Thy ways,
For great and glorious are Thy ways.

UNKNOWN

A Spaceman's Prayer

Father, thank You. . .
Thank You for letting me fly this flight.
Thank You for the privilege of being able to
    be in this position;
to be in this wondrous place, seeing all these
    many startling, wonderful things that You
    have created.
Help, guide, and direct all of us that we may
    shape our lives. . .
trying to help one another and to work with
    one another rather than fighting and
    bickering. . . .
Help us to complete this mission successfully.
Be with all our families. Give them guidance
    and encouragement, and let them know
    that everything will be okay.

L. Gordon Cooper

(From the prayer of Major L. Gordon Cooper,
during his seventeenth orbit, in the middle of
the night over the Indian Ocean.)

GRATITUDE

O Thou, Whose bounty fills my cup
    With every blessing meet!
I give Thee thanks for every drop—
    The bitter and the sweet.
I praise Thee for the desert road,
    And for the riverside;
For all Thy goodness hath bestowed,
    And all Thy grace denied.

JANE CREWDSON

THANKS TO GOD!

Thanks to God for my Redeemer,
  Thanks for all Thou dost provide!
Thanks for times now but a mem'ry,
  Thanks for Jesus by my side!
Thanks for pleasant, balmy springtime,
  Thanks for dark and stormy fall!
Thanks for tears by now forgotten,
  Thanks for peace within my soul!

Thanks for prayers that Thou hast answered,
  Thanks for what Thou dost deny!
Thanks for storms that I have weathered,
  Thanks for all Thou dost supply!
Thanks for pain, and thanks for pleasure,
  Thanks for comfort in despair!
Thanks for grace that none can measure,
  Thanks for love beyond compare!

Thanks for roses by the wayside,
  Thanks for thorns their stems contain!
Thanks for home and thanks for fireside,
  Thanks for hope, that sweet refrain!
Thanks for joy and thanks for sorrow,
  Thanks for heavenly peace with Thee!
Thanks for hope in the tomorrow,
  Thanks through all eternity!

AUGUST LUDVIG STORM

Count Your Blessings

When upon life's billows you are tempest-
    tossed,
When you are discouraged, thinking all is lost,
Count your many blessings—name them one
    by one,
And it will surprise you what the Lord hath
    done.

Are you ever burdened with a load of care?
Does the cross seem heavy you are called to
    bear?
Count your many blessings—every doubt will
    fly,
And you will be singing as the days go by.

When you look at others with their lands and
    gold,
Think that Christ has promised you His wealth
    untold;
Count your many blessings—money cannot buy
Your reward in heaven nor your home on high.

So amid the conflict, whether great or small,
Do not be discouraged—God is over all;
Count your many blessings—angels will attend,
Help and comfort give you to your journey's
    end.

REFRAIN:

Count your blessings—
Name them one by one;
Count your blessings—
See what God hath done;
Count your blessings—
Name them one by one;
Count your many blessings—
See what God hath done.

JOHRSON OATMAN, JR.

*Heavenly Father, help us to see You
in our everyday lives—in the common,
routine things that we do every day—
and help us to recognize You in the unexpected
challenges that arise and catch us off guard.
Help us to trust You at those times!*

Inspirational Library

Beautiful purse/pocket-size editions of Christian classics bound in flexible leatherette. These books make thoughtful gifts for everyone on your list, including yourself!

When I'm on My Knees   The highly popular collection of devotional thoughts on prayer, especially for women.
Flexible Leatherette \$4.97

The Bible Promise Book   Over 1,000 promises from God's Word arranged by topic. What does God promise about matters like: Anger, Illness, Jealousy, Love, Money, Old Age, and Mercy? Find out in this book!
Flexible Leatherette \$3.97

Daily Wisdom for Women   A daily devotional for women seeking biblical wisdom to apply to their lives. Scripture taken from the New American Standard Version of the Bible.
Flexible Leatherette \$4.97

My Daily Prayer Journal   Each page is dated and features a Scripture verse and ample room for you to record your thoughts, prayers, and praises. One page for each day of the year.
Flexible Leatherette \$4.97

Available wherever books are sold.
Or order from:

Barbour Publishing, Inc.
P.O. Box 719
Uhrichsville, OH 44683
http://www.barbourbooks.com

If you order by mail add \$2.00 to your order for shipping.
Prices subject to change without notice.